Great Women in History

Sally Ride

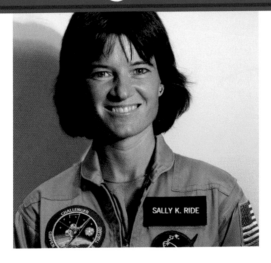

by Erin Edison

Consulting Editor: Gail Saunders-Smith, PhD

CAPSTONE PRESS
a capstone imprint

Pebble Books are published by Capstone Press,
1710 Roe Crest Drive, North Mankato, Minnesota 56003.
www.capstonepub.com

Library of Congress Cataloging-in-Publication Data
Edison, Erin.
Sally Ride / by Erin Edison.
    pages cm.—(Pebble books. Great women in history)
    Summary: "Describes the life and work of Sally Ride, the first American woman in
space"—Provided by publisher.
    Includes bibliographical references and index.
    ISBN 978-1-4765-4215-7 (library binding)—ISBN 978-1-4765-5163-0 (paperback)—
ISBN 978-1-4765-6020-5 (ebook PDF)
    1. Ride, Sally—Juvenile literature. 2. Women astronauts—United States—Biography—
Juvenile literature. 3. Astronauts—United States—Biography—Juvenile literature. I.
Title.
    TL789.85.R53E35 2014
    629.450092—dc23 [B]   2013030097

Editorial Credits

Erika L. Shores, editor; Gene Bentdahl, designer; Marcie Spence, media researcher;
Laura Manthe, production specialist

Photo Credits

Alamy Images: NASA Archive, cover, 4; Corbis: NASA/CNP, 10; NASA: Johnson Space
Center, 1, 12, 14, 16; Newscom: Charles W Lizier/Reuters, 20, Yuri Gripas/Reuters, 18;
Sally Ride: 6

Note to Parents and Teachers

The Great Women in History set supports national social studies standards related to
people and culture. This book describes and illustrates Sally Ride. The images support
early readers in understanding the text. The repetition of words and phrases helps early
readers learn new words. This book also introduces early readers to subject-specific
vocabulary words, which are defined in the Glossary section. Early readers may need
assistance to read some words and to use the Table of Contents, Glossary, Read More,
Internet Sites, and Index sections of the book.

Printed in the United States of America in North Mankato, Minnesota.
092013   007764CGS14

Table of Contents

1951
born

Early Life

Astronaut Sally Ride was the first American woman to travel into space. Sally was born in 1951 in California. Her parents were Dale and Joyce Ride. Sally had a sister named Karen.

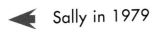
Sally in 1979

 1951
born

1968
graduates
high school

6

Growing up, Sally liked sports.

She was very good at tennis.

Sally thought about playing tennis

as a career after high school.

But she decided to go to college.

She wanted to study science.

Sally played tennis in high school and college.

1951
born

1968
graduates
high school

1978
earns doctoral
degree

Young Adult

Sally studied physics at Stanford University. Physics deals with light, sound, electricity, and other forces. She received a doctoral degree in physics in 1978.

Sally in 1978

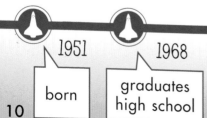

1951
born

1968
graduates
high school

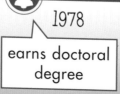

1978
earns doctoral
degree

While at Stanford, Sally found out
NASA was looking for astronauts.
Up until then, women were not
allowed to be astronauts.
Sally applied. She was chosen
by NASA in January 1978.

Sally (far left) and the other women
chosen by NASA in 1978

1951	1968	1978	1978
born	graduates high school	earns doctoral degree	begins astronaut training

12

NASA began training Sally to be an astronaut. She learned how to fly high-speed jets. She also learned more about gravity and how it works in space. She had to learn how to eat and do experiments while floating.

1951 born

1968 graduates high school

1978 earns doctoral degree

1978 begins astronaut training

Life's Work

In 1983 Sally and four other astronauts launched into space aboard the shuttle *Challenger.* For six days Sally and the others did experiments in space. They also released a satellite into space.

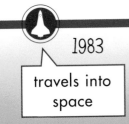

1983

travels into space

1951	1968	1978	1978
born	graduates high school	earns doctoral degree	begins astronaut training

Sally went on her second space flight in 1984. Then in 1986, the *Challenger* exploded after liftoff. Sally was asked to help figure out what went wrong. Sally retired from NASA in 1987.

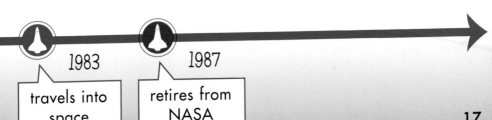

1983
travels into space

1987
retires from NASA

1951	1968	1978	1978
born	graduates high school	earns doctoral degree	begins astronaut training

Later Life

Sally became a physics professor. She worked to encourage students, especially girls, to find science careers. In 2001 she started Sally Ride Science. Her company makes science books and other materials for schools.

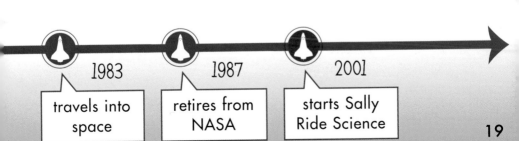

1983
travels into space

1987
retires from NASA

2001
starts Sally Ride Science

1951	1968	1978	1978
born	graduates high school	earns doctoral degree	begins astronaut training

At age 32 Sally was the youngest American to fly in space. She paved the way for female astronauts. Sally died from cancer in 2012. As a teacher she is remembered for encouraging girls to study science.

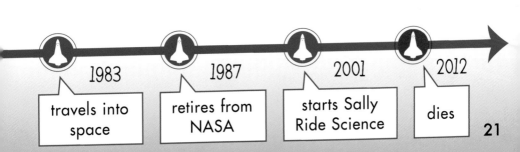

1983
travels into space

1987
retires from NASA

2001
starts Sally Ride Science

2012
dies

Glossary

cancer—a serious disease in which unhealthy cells in the body destroy healthy cells

career—the work or job a person does

doctoral degree—the highest title given to someone for completing a course of study

encourage—to give praise and support

explode—to blow apart with a great force

gravity—a force that pulls objects together

NASA—National Aeronautics and Space Administration; a U.S. government agency that does research on flight and space exploration

physics—science dealing with matter and energy

professor—a teacher with the highest teaching position at a college

retire—to give up a line of work

satellite—a machine circling Earth that gathers and sends information

shuttle—a vehicle that carries astronauts into space and back to Earth

Read More

Braun, Eric. *If I Were an Astronaut.* Dream Big! Minneapolis: Picture Window Books, 2010.

Hamilton, S. L. *Astronaut Firsts.* Xtreme Space. Edina, Minn.: ABDO Pub., 2011.

Royston, Angela. *Astronauts Working in Space.* Big Picture. Mankato, Minn.: Capstone Press, 2010.

Internet Sites

FactHound offers a safe, fun way to find Internet sites related to this book. All of the sites on FactHound have been researched by our staff.

Here's all you do:

Visit *www.facthound.com*

Type in this code: 9781476542157

Check out projects, games and lots more at
www.capstonekids.com

Critical Thinking Using the Common Core

1. Why would someone preparing to become an astronaut need to learn about gravity? (Integration of Knowledge and Ideas)

2. Why do you think NASA chose Sally to help understand why the *Challenger* exploded? (Key Ideas and Details)

Index

Word Count: 295
Grade: 1
Early-Intervention Level: 23